OWEN McCAFFERTY

Born in 1961, Owen lives with his wife and three children
in Belfast. His work includes *Shoot the Crow* (Druid, Galway,
1997); *Mojo Mickybo* (Kabosh, Belfast, 1998); *No Place Like
Home* (Tinderbox, Belfast, 2001); *Closing Time* (National
Theatre, 2002); and *Troubled*, also for the National Theatre.

Owen McCafferty

MOJO MICKYBO

THE WAITING LIST
I WON'T DANCE – DON'T ASK ME

Three Plays

NICK HERN BOOKS
London
www.nickhernbooks.co.uk

A Nick Hern Book

This edition first published in Great Britain in 2002
as a paperback original by Nick Hern Books Limited,
14 Larden Road, London W3 7ST

Mojo Mickybo copyright © 2002 Owen McCafferty
The Waiting List copyright © 2002 Owen McCafferty
I Won't Dance – Don't Ask Me copyright © 2002 Owen McCafferty

Owen McCafferty has asserted his right to be identified as the
author of these works

Typeset by Country Setting, Kingsdown, Kent CT14 8ES
Printed by CLE Print Limited, St Ives, Huntingdon PE27 3LE

ISBN 978 1 85459 701 4

A CIP catalogue record for this book is available from
the British Library

MOJO MICKYBO

For Matthew, Paula and Eoin

Mojo Mickybo was first performed at Andrews Lane Studio, Dublin, on 14 October 1998. The cast was as follows:

MOJO/NARRATOR   Niall Shanahan
MICKYBO   Fergal McElherron

Director Karl Wallace
Designer Terry Loane
Lighting John Riddell
Sound Stephen Handson
Produced by Kabosh Productions

Characters

Mojo Mickybo is a play for two actors. The actors should divide the characters as follows.

MOJO	MICKYBO
Narrator	Fuckface
Gank the Wank	First Woman
Mickybo's Ma	Second Woman
Mickybo's Da	Mojo's Ma
Busman	Mojo's Da
Box Office Woman	Icecream Woman
Torch Woman	The Major
	Uncle Sidney

Note

If possible the actors should be in their late thirties/early forties.

MOJO. mojo

MICKYBO. mickybo

MOJO. mickybo mojo

MICKYBO. mojo mickybo

Mickybo is heading a football against the wall.

NARRATOR. belfast – the summer of 1970 – the heat's meltin the tarmac on the street the buses are burnin bright an punters are drinkin petrol outta milk bottles – this is where mojo an mickybo used to play

MOJO. yer a header mickybo

MICKYBO. gonna bate the record

MOJO. bate it in yer granny's trunks

MICKYBO. yer granny's trunks – mickybo's the man – bate five hundred an twenty-nine – roun to gank the wank an spit in his eye

MOJO. dig ye he will

MICKYBO. bate that gank – spit in his big rubber eye

MOJO. many ya done?

MICKYBO. a hundred an twenty-three – twenty-four – twenty-five . . .

MOJO. mickybo flat head

MICKYBO. onion dome

MOJO. barney rip the balls comes out you'll be onion dome

MICKYBO. comes near me i'll boot his cat up the hole

MOJO. would ye?

MICKYBO. aye – big hairy boot right up the hole an into the lagan

MOJO. get ye with that big knife cut the gizzard outta ye

MICKYBO. i'll cut the gizzard outta him – see when he's lyin there with no gizzard i'll spit in his good eye an gliss his chops

MOJO. he comes out that door you'll shit yerself

MICKYBO. you'll shit yerself – you always shit yerself

MOJO. you do

MICKYBO. you do

MOJO. kack the breeks

MICKYBO. shit the trunks

NARRATOR. mojo mickybo – thick as two small thieves – the greatest lads god ever pumped breath into – the day they met was the hottest ever in the whole of christendom – the sweats drippin from the trees an dogs are jumpin off bridges in the hope they can fly – the world draggin itself along like it was out of breath – a belter

MOJO. many ya done now mickybo?

MICKYBO. three hundred an twenty-four – twenty-five – twenty-six . . .

MOJO. yer arse is in america

MICKYBO. ganko the wanko over an outo

MOJO. barneyo ripo the ballso

MICKYBO. barneyo no gizzardo

NARRATOR. that day wee mojo was on his own – an empty type of a day – the type a day you'd kick stones an chalk yer name on a wall rather than listen to yer ma an da spittin bullets at each other – that type of a day – know what a mean

MOJO. many now mickybo?

MICKYBO. four hundred an thirty-six – thirty-seven – thirty-eight – mojo?

MOJO. wha?

MICKYBO. how d'ya stop a biafran from drownin?

NARRATOR. throw him a polo mint

MICKYBO. throw him a polo mint

MOJO. polo mints are catmalogion

MICKYBO. catmalogion – sherbert dips

MOJO. weeker

MICKYBO. weeker

NARRATOR. after danderin here there an nowhere mojo foun himself in the park – an for the want of somethin to do he just lay on his back an looked up at the sky thinkin to himself – that if he were a giant that ate clouds he'd starve on days like this – an the only place they could bury him would be the park

MOJO. ya done yet mickybo?

MICKYBO. five hundred an thirty (*He stops heading.*) told ye told ye told ye – gank the wank bate by mickybo – five hundred an thirty headers – the bo – the lad – barney rip the balls' backdoor

NARRATOR. kick kick kick – blatter blatter blatter

MICKYBO. barney rip the balls picks his arse with a big fishbone – yer cat's a dead man – offski

NARRATOR. so we're there – the first day – mojo an mickybo – mickybo's sittin on the groun under a big dead tree diggin a hole in the dirt with a stick – mojo's standin lookin

MICKYBO. what ya lookin at?

MOJO. nothin

MICKYBO. i'm diggin a hole with a stick – might find somethin

MOJO. like wha?

MICKYBO. don't know haven't foun it yet – treasure maybe – i'm hidin as well like – you hidin?

MOJO. nah – rollin down the hill

MICKYBO. weeker – i'm hidin from gank the wank an fuckface – ya see em?

MOJO. nah don't know em

MICKYBO. i hate them – ugly bastards – stole my bike – a chopper – gears an everythin it had – said they didn't but the did – know barney rip the balls?

MOJO. nah

MICKYBO. everybody knows rip the balls – he puts black boot polish in his hair an doesn't wear no socks – an my da says he pisses in the sink cause he couldn't be fucked to go out to the yard – nobody's ever saw im but me – i saw im buryin dead rats over the timbers – wanna dig with the stick?

MOJO. aye

MICKYBO. if yer ball goes into his yard he slits it with a big knife an ya never get it back – i kicked fuckface's ball into his yard cause he stole my bike – big knife in fuckface's ball – now they're after me – if ya sat here all summer ya could dig yer way to australia

MOJO. aye – or china

MICKYBO. what's yer name?

MOJO. mojo

MICKYBO. i'm mickybo – mojo mickybo mickybo mojo – sounds like a gang – where ya from?

MOJO. up the road – where you from?

MICKYBO. over the bridge – you go to school up the road?

MOJO. aye

MICKYBO. i hate school – gank an fuckface always get their gang to chase me roun the yard

MOJO. school's wick – except lunchtime – go over the brickies an have sand fights

MICKYBO. can ya fight?

MOJO. i kicked applegoat up the balls once cause he farted in my face – hairy dan slapped me

MICKYBO. me an you could be against gank the wank an fuckface – you could kick em up the balls

MOJO. are the big?

MICKYBO. ugly big bastards – me an you bate them though – get them one at a time kick em up the balls

MOJO. aye – alright

MICKYBO. you'll have to swear on it

MOJO. i swear on my granny's eyes i'm the enemy of gank the wank an fuckface

MICKYBO. if ya break the swear her eyes'll explode

MOJO. aye

MICKYBO. ya wanna roll down the hill

MOJO. rollin down the hill's weeker

MICKYBO. last to the bottom stinks a shite

NARRATOR. the lads rolled down the hill for two days an then went to the pictures – the saturday mornin club

MOJO / MICKYBO. good morning uncle sidney

UNCLE SIDNEY (*showman*). good morning children

MOJO / MICKYBO. big smiles for yer uncle sidney

UNCLE SIDNEY. get yer smelly kebs off that seat or i'll bust yer fuckin arse

MOJO / MICKEYBO. sorry uncle sidney

MOJO. where ya goin mickybo?

MICKYBO. crawl under the seats up to the front an fire cola cubes up at batman's head

MOJO. torchwoman'll get ye – tell yer ma

MICKYBO. i'll use the anti-torchwoman bat gun

MOJO. hollygwaockamoly batman not the anti-torchwoman bat gun

MICKYBO. it's the only way robin – it's either that or bate her with the torch

TORCHWOMAN (*speaks slowly and chews gum*). uncle sidney they're messin in the back stalls an they've their smelly kebs up on the good seats

MICKYBO. her light is blindin me boy wonder – fire the anti-torchwoman bat gun

MOJO (*fires the gun*). the gas is everywhere escape to the batcave

TORCHWOMAN. come back here ya wee toerags – uncle sidney uncle sidney they're torturin me uncle sidney – they have ma head turned

MICKYBO. the fat bitch is still alive robin hit her with a nailbomb

MOJO (*throws a nailbomb*). the light shines no more

TORCHWOMAN (*raising her hand*). i'll swing for ye's ye's wee buggers (*Smooths her skirt.*) yes uncle sidney comin now big boy

UNCLE SIDNEY (*unzips his trousers*). uncle sidney loves the saturday morning club – put that torch out

MICKYBO. the batcave boy wonder

NARRATOR. the batcave – that would be the place to be alright – god's fear never crossin the door an every livin dead thing killed usin nothin more than a bag of cola cubes – the type of place ya could hold yer own spit forever

Cheeks bloated. Mickybo indicates they should bend over the balcony and empty their spit on the people below. They do this and then quickly pull back and sit in their seats.

MICKYBO. i had more spit than you

MOJO. no ya didn't

MICKYBO. aye a did

MOJO. no ya didn't

MICKYBO. aye a did

NARRATOR. back in the sunlight – sittin on the curb outside the pictures – watchin the soldiers stoppin cars an chewin the rest of the cola cubes

MOJO. the sun makin yer sweets stick together?

MICKYBO. aye

MOJO. i like em like that

MICKYBO. weeker – i ate the paper on em

MOJO. on everythin?

MICKYBO. except chews – ya couldn't ate chew paper – ever go to the flicktures at night?

MOJO. wouldn't let ye in

MICKYBO. aye the would

MOJO. no the wouldn't

MICKYBO. go tonight

MOJO. to see wha?

MICKYBO. that

A poster. They take up the positions of Butch Cassidy and the Sundance Kid *on the poster, ie running forward guns blazing.*

butch cassidy an the sundance kid – cowboys

They circle each other as gunfighters.

MICKYBO. where ya from mister?

MOJO. i'm a stranger in these parts boy

MICKYBO. i know that ya geek ye

They giggle.

MOJO. i'm from outta town

MICKYBO. we don't like outta towners – you gotta name stranger?

MOJO. banana trunks

MICKYBO. you ever hear of a gunslinger called pele – banana trunks – that's me

MOJO. you wanna draw pele banana trunks?

They burst out laughing.

MICKYBO. draw pele banana trunks

MOJO. sharpen yer crayon banana trunks

Still laughing Mickybo fires shots into the air.

NARRATOR. butch cassidy an the sundance kid – a fine feelin it must be to be a cowboy – money in yer pocket a horse on yer arse an a gun in yer holster – but times are hard – there's no ham for the sandwiches an torchwoman is in the box office payin her dues – a wee dab behind the ears of the da's aftershave for mojo and mickbyo – just to smell the part

They push each other forward.

MICKYBO. no you

MOJO. no you

They straighten up to look older and take on deep voices.

MICKYBO. two tickets for the frontstalls to see the cowboy movie butch cassidy an the sundance kid – thank you

BOX OFFICE WOMAN. they're back again uncle sidney – the wee friggers are back again

MICKYBO. two tickets for the frontstalls to see the cowboy movie butch cassidy an the sundance kid – thank you

BOX OFFICE WOMAN. uncle sidney they're torturin me – slap the lugs off them for me

MICKYBO. look missus see if we don't get in i'm gonna stand outside an tell everyone we saw ye lumberin uncle sidney

MOJO (*exaggerated kissing*). we spied ye

BOX OFFICE WOMAN. a woman's allowed a wee bitta comfort in the world – ya don't know what it's like – my man's mean an stinkin – go up to the front circle (*Angry.*) sidney get yer fat sweaty arse over here

They watch the movie and eat sweets. Big smiles.

NARRATOR (*sings*). don't ever hit your granny with a shovel, it leaves a dull impression on her mind – what happens mickybo when ya hit yer granny with a shovel?

MICKYBO. her eyes pop out an her face goes like that (*Grimace.*)

NARRATOR. butch an sundance blazin a trail – no finer men

MICKYBO. no finer men

NARRATOR. glued to the screen – fightin every battle – shootin every shot – an always rootin for the good guys

MICKYBO. don't go up the mountain butch they get ye if ya go up the mountain (*Fires a gun.*)

NARRATOR. half time – back to the real world – decisions have to be made – important decisions that would give a book a headache – who's who an what's what

MICKYBO. yer sundance i'm butch

MOJO. why?

MICKYBO. just

MOJO. just why?

MICKYBO. just cause

MOJO. just cause why?

MICKYBO. just cause i say so

MOJO. i baggsie Butch

MICKYBO. ya can't

MOJO. a can

MICKYBO. i'll buy ya an icecream

MOJO. anythin you say butch

MICKYBO. fine with me sundance

NARRATOR. icecream in bake gun in mit an we're sailin back into the wild west – a place where there's no traffic lights – men drink beer from buckets – an nobody gives a tuppenny fig if horses shite in the street

They sit and watch. Eyes wide open. They react to every shot fired on the screen without leaving their seats.

MICKYBO. that was fuckin weeker

NARRATOR. the war's over an now butch an sundance have to stand for the queen

Mickybo twirls his guns and fires them in the air. Mojo stands to attention. They make funny faces and wave bye-bye.

MICKYBO. bye bye uncle sidney (*Exaggerated kissing.*)

MOJO. uncle sidney lumbers big seven bellies (*Firing guns.*)

MICKYBO. mcmanus luiga riva

MOJO. s o s dannybobo

MICKYBO. don del a vista

NARRATOR. from the dim light into the dark night an straight into gank the wank an fuckface

MICKYBO. gank – fuckface

FUCKFACE. you owe me a ball mickybo

MICKYBO. where's my bike fuckface?

FUCKFACE. we haven't got yer smelly bike

MICKYBO. aye ya have – it had gears an everything

FUCKFACE. we got his bike gank?

GANK. didn't touch it fuckface

FUCKFACE. my da bate me cause the ball was lost – didn't he bate me gank?

GANK. the tubes right outta ye fuckface

FUCKFACE. i get another ball or i'm gonna dig ye – it was the same one the used in the world cup

GANK. except it was plastic fuckface

Fuckface slaps Gank.

FUCKFACE. the used them in the world cup

GANK. world cup fuckface

FUCKFACE. who's yer mate?

MICKYBO. mojo

FUCKFACE. where ya from?

MICKYBO. leave im alone – nothin to do with you where he's from

FUCKFACE. where ya from?

GANK. aye where ya from?

MICKYBO. say nothin mojo

FUCKFACE. fuck up – ya hear me – where ya from?

MOJO. up the road

FUCKFACE. up the road where?

MOJO. up the road up the road

FUCKFACE. funny fucker are ye

MOJO. no

FUCKFACE. me an my da chases the ones up the road – afeared of us they are – i don't like you – do you like him gank?

GANK. no fuckface

FUCKFACE. any odds? – give us yer odds or ya have to fight us

MICKYBO. kick im up the balls mojo (*No one moves.*) go on mojo kick im up the balls

FUCKFACE. come on

MICKYBO. mcmanus luigi riva – don del a vista – flamenco – bingo

NARRATOR. mojo an mickybo (*Bat wings fluttering.*) down the road like bats out a hell

MICKYBO. the stopped chasin us?

MOJO. aye (*Gun out.*) butch?

MICKYBO. wha?

MOJO. who are those guys?

MICKYBO. who are those guys?

MOJO. i was gonna kick im up the balls mickybo a was

MICKYBO. i was gonna stick ma fingers in his ears pull im down an boot im up the hole – we'll do them the next time – next time we'll do them

MOJO. aye up the balls an the hole – s o s danny bobo

MICKYBO. don del a vista – member?

MOJO. wha?

MICKYBO. see if ya hit yer granny with a shovel (*Grimace.*)

NARRATOR. mojo galloped back up the road thinkin mickybo was a geg (*Sings.*) rain drops keep fallin on my head – because i'm free nothin worrin me – mojo lifts a stick from the bonfire at the top of his street – can i move i'm better when i move – bang bang bang bang – the woman at the top of his street – fluffy slippers wee legs tight skits an big fegs – big moustaches – all dead as doornails

MOJO. yous are dead – i'm the sundance kid an yous are dead

The two women continuously smoke. One inhales the other exhales.

FIRST WOMAN. wee mojo – yer a duck egg for yer da – isn't he a duck egg for his da?

SECOND WOMAN. duck egg

MOJO. i'm not wee mojo i'm the sundance kid an yous are dead – bang bang bang bang – i was at the flicktures and saw the cowboy movie butch cassidy an the sundance kid – ever been to the flicktures?

FIRST WOMAN. oh uncle sidney

SECOND WOMAN. big uncle sidney

FIRST WOMAN. member uncle sidney

SECOND WOMAN. he was the boy alright

FIRST WOMAN. good mornin uncle sidney

SECOND WOMAN. night night uncle sidney

MOJO. uncle sidney's a tube – me an mickybo shot him dead – we're real cowboys

FIRST WOMAN. yer like my man he's a real cowboy

SECOND WOMAN. all men are cowboys

MOJO. like butch an sundance?

FIRST WOMAN. aye but not as good lookin

SECOND WOMAN. we need good lookin cowboys mojo – ya know any?

FIRST WOMAN. you could be our good lookin cowboy mojo – we could all live on a big ranch – it would be lovely

MOJO. i'm not mojo i'm the sundance kid an yous are dead – bang bang bang bang – have to go now have to see ma ma

FIRST WOMAN. if ya see any good lookin cowboys won't ya tell us

MOJO. bang bang bang bang – alright ma – anythin to eat ma?

MOJO'S MA. there's a tin a pineapple chunks in the cupboard

MOJO. i'm the sundance kid ma

MOJO'S MA. are ya that's good

MOJO. pineapple chunks for the sundance kid – the women up the street ma say all men are cowboys – is my da a cowboy ma – me an him could be cowboys together couldn't we ma

MOJO'S MA. aye son

MOJO. do ya want pineapple chunks ma?

MOJO'S MA. no son

MOJO. where's my da ma?

MOJO'S MA. in there gettin ready to go out

MOJO. i'm the best shot in the wild west ma – throw yer feg up in the air an i'll shoot it ma

MOJO'S MA. away into the house mojo

MOJO. you lookin up at the sky ma – the sky all red ma – why's the sky all red ma?

MOJO'S MA. something's burnin

MOJO. what's burnin ma?

MOJO'S MA. i don't know

MOJO. call me sundance ma

MOJO'S MA. away into the house sundance

MOJO. sundance is away in to ate his pineapple chunks ma (*Eating from a tin.*) – pineapple chunks da?

MOJO'S DA. no son a don't want any pineapple chunks

MOJO. you goin out da?

MOJO'S DA. aye son i'm goin out

MOJO. where ya goin? – ya goin dancin again da?

MOJO'S DA. aye i'm goin dancin

MOJO. ya must like dancin da – do you like dancin da?

MOJO'S DA. aye son i like dancin

MOJO. do ya dance on yer on da – ya always go dancin on yer own

MOJO'S DA. yer ma doesn't like dancin that's why

MOJO. my ma likes smokin da

MOJO'S DA. aye

MOJO. me an mickybo are butch cassidy an the sundance kid da – mickybo's my new mate da

MOJO'S DA. is he that's good

MOJO. the women up the street da say all men are cowboys da – me you an mickybo are three cowboys

MOJO'S DA. cowboys – aye

MOJO. can i go dancin with ya da?

MOJO'S DA. no son dancin's only for big people

MOJO. the men does the dancin an the wee lads ate the pineapple chunks – that right da?

MOJO'S DA. aye

NARRATOR. a lot a smokin a wee bit a jivin an there's sad songs in the air – the ring is round the church is square i drank the giro why weren't you there – enough of that says mojo – mickybo's house – blatter blatter blatter – is mickybo in mickybo's ma

MICKYBO'S MA. no son he's not – he's gone – it's a sad bad thing but we had to do it there was no way out of it – i was cooking a big pot of stew for us all – a big pot the size of a buffalo's head – enough stew to do us for a month and a day – i was stirring the stew with the shaft of a brush and the gas went out – panic hit the air – the man i love header and all as he is mickybo's da had a thirst on him that stretched the length and breadth of ireland – and god bless the weak and distraught man that he is in a fit of madness due to the sun had blew the last few shillings we had on bad drink – drink so bad that it made his feet stink and his eyes roll about in his head like they were lost – what can ya do when yer man needs fed an him that would ate a large child's arse through a small rope chair – and you couldn't hand him half cooked stew for fear of him choking on the hard bits – him not bein able to chew that well – just in the nick a time a gypsy man called to the door wantin to sell me some carpet – i told him we didn't need carpet we needed money for the gas – how much for the youngster he said – enough to let me finish cooking the stew i said – it broke my heart but what has to be done has to be done – i sold wee mickybo to the gypsies so i could cook a pot of stew

Mojo's mouth open – agog.

MOJO. yer a geg mickybo's ma – mickybo yer ma's a geg

MICKYBO. she's a tube

MICKYBO'S MA. my wee honeybun (*She ruffles Mickybo's hair.*)

MICKYBO. wise up ma will ye – give us some money ma

MICKYBO'S MA. the man i love header and all as he is has all the money son – away up an rob him

NARRATOR. butch an sundance mossied up the street an straight into the saloon

They push saloon doors open.

MICKYBO. ma ma says you've to give us some money

MICKYBO'S DA. money is it – what makes ya think i've any money

MICKYBO. ya need money to buy beer

MICKYBO'S DA. talk's cheap but ya need readies to buy gargle

MICKYBO. we're cowboys da

MICKYBO'S DA. cowboys is it – an where are the cowboys for today?

MICKYBO. bolivia

MICKYBO'S DA. that would be the place to go alright – anywhere but this kip – what about australia – gooday gooday gooday digga

MICKYBO. butch an sundance were gonna go to australia but then they got shot so they didn't go

MICKYBO'S DA. gooday gooday gooday digga – yer ma has a brother out there – an eejit like but doin alright for himself – australia – be better than this fuckin kip – what do ya think son – think we should all go to australia?

MICKYBO. can mojo go?

MICKYBO'S DA. aye why not we'll all fuck off to australia – gooday gooday gooday digga

MICKYBO. wanna go to australia mojo?

MOJO. i'll have to ask ma ma – ma me an mickybo's goin to australia – mickybo's da's takin us – mickybo's ma has a brother out there – he's an eejit but he's doin alright for himself

MOJO'S MA (*smoking*). that's great son just make sure yer back before tea

MICKYBO. ma?

MICKYBO'S MA. my wee honeybun

MICKYBO. ma da says we're all goin to australia ma

MICKYBO'S MA. yer da says more than his prayers son

MICKYBO. do you say more than yer prayers da?

MICKYBO'S DA (*drunk*). she'd fuckin know wouldn't she – knows fuck all about fuck all – i'll get us there alright – me on ma swanny – i'll fuckin do it alright – don't you worry about that – no sweat about it

MICKYBO. no sweat about it da

MICKYBO'S DA. no sweat about it is right an don't you think any fuckin different – i don't need no fucker to tell me or help me or fuck all else – brother in australia fuck im – he was a wanker when he was here an he's a wanker out there – it's not meant to be like this son – sort everythin out – fuck away off out a this kip – ya understan that do ye?

MICKYBO. no da a don't

MICKYBO'S DA. no da a don't – aye well ya should

MICKYBO. will a understan when we're in australia da?

MICKYBO'S DA. fuck australia an everyone in it – what the fuck would they know

MICKYBO. gooday gooday gooday digga da

MICKYBO'S DA. gooday ma ballix (*Collapses.*)

MOJO. mickybo yer da's a geg

MICKYBO. aye he's a geg – mon we'll poke sticks into barney rip the balls' cat

MOJO. here pussy pussy – here pussy pussy

MICKYBO. pish wish wish wish wish wish wish – i heard he carries a knife the length of a monkey's arm

MOJO. a monkey's arm?

MICKYBO. aye – puss puss puss – i heard he keeps the cat in a box an only lets it out to ate rats

MOJO. ever see his cat?

MICKYBO. nah – do ya think he's ate it?

MOJO. ate his own cat

MICKYBO. aye

MOJO. is that him up at the winda

MICKYBO (*shouts*). ate the cat – barny rip the balls ate the cat

MOJO (*shouts*). ate the pussy rip the balls

MICKYBO. butch an sundance offski – there's gank on his own mon we'll get im

MOJO. mcmanus luigi riva

MICKYBO. where's my bike gank?

GANK. i don't know nothin about yer smelly bike

MICKYBO. where's fuckface?

GANK. over at the launderette doin his ma's washin

MICKYBO. doin yer ma's washin means yer a tube – yer our prisoner so ya do as we say or mojo'll kick ya up the balls an i'll bout ya up the hole – give us somethin

GANK. i have nothin

MICKYBO. stan a hoke

Mickybo searches Gank.

fegs mojo

MOJO. fegs mickybo

GANK. there fuckface's fegs he'll kill me

MOJO. hardwire Gank

MICKYBO. hardwire gank – tell im butch an sundance took his fegs an if he wants to know where to get us we'll be in bolivia

MOJO. or australia

MICKYBO. or australia – go an tell im tell im when he's finished he can do my ma's washin

GANK. nobody likes you mickybo and yer da's full a mad dog's keek (*He spits at Mickybo then runs away.*)

MICKYBO. will we ran after him or have a smoke?

MOJO. have a smoke

They check all is clear and then light up.

MICKYBO. you ever smoke before?

MOJO. nah

They cough.

MICKYBO. magic

MOJO. weeker

They blow smoke into the air.

MICKYBO. t'morrow we'll go roun to square head mcguckian's an steal fegs an bubblies – smoke all day

MOJO. i've to go out with ma da t'morrow

MICKYBO. out where with ye da?

MOJO. i can't tell ye it's a secret – he told me a can't tell

MICKYBO. ya can't have secrets if yer in a gang – ya have to tell

MOJO. we always go to the park an he gives me a swing – push higher da

MOJO'S DA. always higher – you've my back broke wee lad – should be swingin yerself the age a ya

MOJO. higher da higher

MOJO'S DA. we've to go for the icecream – we can't be late for the icecream

MOJO. after the swings we walk into town an ma da buys me an icecream

MOJO'S DA. sit down an behave the girl'll bring the icecream over now

MOJO. you not gonna sit with me da?

MOJO'S DA. i've to go an do a message – just sit there an eat yer icecream an not a word out a ye

MICKYBO. what flavour do ya get? do ya get bubbly flavour?

MOJO. nah – strawberry

MICKYBO. strawberry's alright but bubbly's better

MOJO. see when i've finished my icecream i get another one

ICECREAM WOMAN. (*Slow.*) there's another icecream – mind ya don't get any on yer good shirt – yer da says yer allowed thee – i think thee ice creams is too much for a wee lad – my man ates anythin but he wouldn't ate thee ice creams – yer da has ya spoilt rotten

MOJO. after the three icecreams ma da's back from doin his message – where'd ya go da?

MOJO'S DA. didn't a say i had a message to do – well that what a was doin

MOJO. what message da?

MOJO'S DA. never you mind – nothin that concerns you

MOJO. he gives the woman the money for the icecream an then the two a them laugh

They laugh – ha ha ha.

next week da can we bring ma ma with us – she can sit with me while yer away doin yer message

MOJO'S DA. no she's not to know about this – ya understan? this is our wee secret

MOJO. why da?

MOJO'S DA. do ya understan – i'm warnin ye now say nothin

MOJO. why da?

MOJO'S DA. cause i say so that's why

MOJO. okay da

MOJO'S DA. look son if yer ma knew you were eatin icecream before yer dinner wouldn't she do her nut

MOJO. she would do her nut da

MOJO'S DA. that's why it has to be a secret

MOJO. right da – can we go to the swings on the way home da?

MOJO'S DA. straight home for dinner i'm starvin

MOJO. if ya ate the icecream like me ya wouldn't be starvin da

MICKYBO. does yer da not ate icecream?

MOJO. nah

MICKYBO. that's borin – yer da's borin mojo – mon we'll go
over the timbers an burn wood

MOJO. aye

They strike a match – whoof.

MICKYBO. wanna know what i heard?

MOJO. wha?

MICKYBO. the whole a belfast is goin mad an we're all gonna
get murdered in our beds

MOJO. where'd ya hear that?

MICKYBO. barney rip the balls

MOJO. you see him?

MICKYBO. nah – a was spittin through his letterbox an he
shouted down the stairs – runnin about lookin for his big
knife he was – he shouted fuck off an leave my letterbox
alone – then he shouted belfast was mad an we're all gettin
murdered in our beds

MOJO. all of us?

MICKYBO. everybody – ya couldn't get murdered in yer bed
if ya weren't in it so we'll build a hut over the timbers an
live in it

MOJO. all of us?

MICKYBO. think he's right?

MOJO. a don't know

MICKYBO (*pushes open saloon door*). da are we all goin get
murdered in our beds?

MICKYBO'S DA (*drinking*). gooday gooday gooday digga –
murdered in yer bed is it – that type a crack wouldn't
happen to ye if ya were roamin the outback shootin
kangaroos for a livin an drinkin soup from a billy can

MICKYBO. aye da billy can – ma i think we should all move
out of the house an live in a hut me an mojo made over the
timbers – there's plenty of room – there's nothin in it but a

rubber bullet – the brits fired it down the street durin the riotin an i nabbed it – plenty a room ma – we'll all be safe in the hut ma

MICKYBO'S MA. would you like to hear my plan son – i was sittin on top of a mountain of dishes the other night listening to elvis on the radio and thinking of the time when the man that i love header and all that he is used to take me dancing – (*Sings.*) oh how we danced on the night we were wed we danced and we danced cause the room had no bed – there was this strange noise come out of the radio it sounded like the king had eaten something very large that didn't agree with him and was choking on his own boke – then a voice said we come in peace earth people – then the voice said don't lose your heads earth people if you lose your head you lose your money – things may be gettin a bit hairy but we're here to save you all especially wee mickybo mickybo's ma an the man that she loves header and all that he is – we're shippin you out to a planet where there's no dishes the stew makes itself the sky rains beer and the hills are made of bubblies – so we're alright wee honeybun – we don't need to live in the hut that you and mojo built over the timbers – cause the spacemen are coming to save us

MICKYBO. very funny ma

MOJO. yer ma's a geg mickybo

MICKYBO. if we all get murdered in our beds it'll be yer fault ma cause we're not in the hut

MICKYBO'S MA (*ruffles Mickybo's hair*). my wee honeybun

MICKYBO. ask yer ma an da

MOJO. da

MOJO'S DA. get a good shine on them boy – ya can tell the cut of a man by the shine on his shoes

MOJO. aye da

MOJO'S DA. yer a good kid

MOJO. aye da – ma

No answer.

MOJO. the sun's splittin the trees ma – will a open the curtains?

MOJO'S MA. no son

MOJO. do ya think we should live in a hut ma?

MOJO'S MA. just me an you son?

MOJO. and my da an mickybo an his ma an da – they're a geg ma

MOJO'S MA. no son i don't think we should live in a hut

MOJO. right ma – i'm away out to play now – butch an sundance an the hut an the rubber bullet – mcmanus luigi riva ma

NARRATOR. we played and sat in the hut waitin on the worst

They smoke a cigarette between them.

MICKYBO. don't be puttin a duck's arse on it

MOJO. duck's arse me arse

MICKYBO. if everything was to burn down what would ya do?

MOJO (*hosing*). be a fireman

MICKYBO. fireman be catmalogion

MOJO. fireman be class

MICKYBO. my da says he read in a book that the fires in australia last for weeks and that postmen fly planes an earn a fuckin fortune

MICKYBO'S DA. gooday gooday gooday digga – postman in australia uses planes – must be on a fuckin fortune – we're all goin to australia – remember that mickybo the whole fuckin lot of us

MICKYBO. aye da the whole fuckin lot of us

They blow smoke in the air.

MICKYBO. if i can spit out the hole in that plank you owe me a marley

MOJO. plank ma tubes

MICKYBO. i spit the best in our street

MOJO. if ya miss you've to give me yer catty

MICKYBO. a marley for a catty – peel a grape an ate a bap – a catty's worth five marleys

MOJO. yer big hole

MICKYBO. no bet – a bet ye a can do it though

MOJO. welt on walter

MICKYBO. i got morons on my team goddamn morons on my team (*Mickybo spits.*) – mickybo is the spit master – bet ye i can spit an hit that nail

MICKYBO. i'm meltin mon we'll throw skimmers

They throw skimmers across the river.

MICKYBO. ya think australia be like this?

MOJO. like wha?

MICKYBO. throwin skimmers over the river

MOJO. aye

MICKYBO. bet ye Australia's weeker – bet ye the all go to school on horses

MOJO. do ya really wanna go to australia?

MICKYBO. aye – ya could get blown up here – that be cat

MOJO. a wee lad in our school was in town with his ma an a bomb went off – an it blew one of his legs off

MICKYBO. right off in one go like?

MOJO. aye – but his trousers was still on him

MICKYBO. if ya foun his leg ya could sew it on to ye – three legs – keep the ball up forever

MOJO. what would ya do if ya went to australia an there was bombs there too

MICKYBO. why would there be bombs there?

MOJO. don't know

MICKYBO. get my da to take us somewhere else

MOJO. i'd like to go to america

MICKYBO. is australia near america?

MOJO. aye – they're connected by a bridge or somethin

MICKYBO. if ya went to america an i went to australia it would be like now – yer up the road an i'm over the bridge

MOJO. if superman was here there'd be no bombs

MICKYBO. aye he'd hear them tickin with his x-ray ears

MOJO. then he could just zoom down pick it up an throw it into space – everythin's safe there cause there's nothin to blow up in space

MICKYBO. batman couldn't do that

MOJO. batman be useless in belfast

MICKYBO. he'd be too slow – he has to use the batmobile an ya have to fly if ya wanna save bombs

MOJO. superman would've saved that wee lad in our school but batman wouldn't – what about spiderman he swings from buildins?

MICKYBO. he couldn't throw a bomb into space

MOJO. he could cover it in a web and then when it went off nothin would happen

MICKYBO. does superman go to australia?

MOJO. nah he only saves america

MICKYBO. maybe australia has their own

MOJO. kangarooman

MICKYBO. he'd put the bomb in his hole then bounce off into the bushes

MOJO. aye – think they'll blow the bridge up?

MICKYBO. what would ya do if they did blow the bridge up?

MOJO. weeker – i could stay in yer house

MICKYBO. aye that be weeker – everyone have to swim to work wouldn't they

MOJO. i hope they do blow the bridge up

MICKYBO. big bomb the size of a house blow it up

MOJO. dynamite like butch an sundance used – quick we've only ten seconds before the bridge blows – take cover

MICKYBO. oh no the fuse has gone out

MOJO. what will we do?

MICKYBO. we have to save the city – stop everybody gettin murdered in their beds

MOJO. we need a volunteer soldier

MICKYBO. i'm the major yer the soldier

MOJO. i'm not doin it i'm too young to die – i have a wife an a shitload of kids

MICKYBO. it's an order soldier – if we're gonna save the city the bridge must go an yer gonna have to go with it

MOJO. have i a last request?

MICKYBO. yes

MOJO. it has to happen – it's a last request so it must happen

MICKYBO. yes goddamn it man yes

MOJO. i want you to die with me

MICKYBO. alright

MOJO. we're dying to save the city

MICKYBO. light the fuse soldier

Mojo lights the fuse. Mickybo salutes. The bridge explodes and so do they.

NARRATOR. the bridge didn't blow – so after smokin their last fegs in the hut an watchin the river slip away mojo crossed the bridge and walked home – he didn't really want to go home but his stomach was empty so home it was – he walked slowly – the heat drew people out of their houses – they stood on street corners chewin the fat – those that didn't chew the fat hung flags an bunting an painted the kerbs – the heat – the people – the colour – it was a party – a party so big that no buildin could hold it so it spilled out onto the streets – the major was guardin the bonfire – a big heavy overcoat – the sweat lashin – the wine guzzlin – an wasps buzzin aroun his mouth

THE MAJOR (*swiping wasps away*). it's the wine – the wasps is after the wine

MOJO. why ya wearin a coat when it's hot major?

THE MAJOR. always carry everything ya own wee man – never know when ya have to jump ship

MOJO. you mindin the bonfire major?

THE MAJOR. that's the job give to me – big bottle a wine for the major

MOJO. the gonna steal the bonfire major?

THE MAJOR. god bless the bonfire wee man – big bottle a wine

MOJO. you gonna sleep in the bonfire major?

THE MAJOR. i am – never let it be said the major wouldn't sleep in a bonfire when he was bid

MOJO. i'm away home now major

THE MAJOR. god bless ulster wee man

MOJO. except the wasps major – ya wouldn't want god to bless the wasps

THE MAJOR. after the wine – bastards

NARRATOR. just before he left mojo shot the major dead –
    bang bang bang bang – yer a dead man major – the street
    was alive – standin up straight – its face bright and shiny –
    an all the while the sun's beamin down

MOJO. do wasps drink wine da? – the major says wasps drink
    wine da

Silence.

the major's funny da he eats wasps and lives inside the
    bonfire – you cut yer hand da?

MOJO'S DA. a hit the wall a punch son

MOJO. what ya do that for da?

MOJO'S DA. i don't know

MOJO. ya shouldn't do things like that da

MOJO'S DA. no a shouldn't

MOJO. my ma's not standin at the front door da – where is
    she?

MOJO'S DA. she's up the stairs – i wanna talk to you about
    somethin mojo

MOJO. what da?

Silence.

MOJO'S DA. nothin – away up to yer ma see she's alright

MOJO. are wasps bees da?

MOJO'S DA. away up to yer ma mojo

MOJO. are wasps bees ma?

MOJO'S MA. me an yous gonna stay with yer auntie rita for
    awhile mojo

MOJO. why ma?

MOJO'S MA. a wee holiday – ya like yer auntie rita don't ya

MOJO. no ma – she stinks a bleach and pinches my face – is
    ma da not goin?

MOJO'S MA. just me an you mojo

MOJO. i don't wanna go ma

MOJO'S MA. yer not stayin here with him – yer comin with me

NARRATOR. mojo's ma packed a suitcase while his da stood and looked on in silence

MOJO (*trailed by the hand*). there's the women smokin in the street ma (*Shouts to women.*) we're goin on holidays – me an ma ma an a suitcase

FIRST WOMAN. away anywhere nice mojo?

MOJO. auntie rita's

SECOND WOMAN. the weather'll be lovely there

FIRST WOMAN. send us a postcard

SECOND WOMAN. bring us back a good lookin cowboy

The women laugh.

MOJO. the smokin women want a good lookin cowboy ma

MOJO'S MA. stop talkin mojo

NARRATOR. mojo thought havin banter with the women was funny – his ma didn't – she had other things on her mind – things she thought but didn't speak – they walked the rest of the way in silence two suitcases draggin behind them – after a few days of his ma's fegs an auntie rita's bleach it was time for mickybo's – the major had shifted camp – guardin the bonfire at the top of auntie rita's street now

THE MAJOR. the wee soldier laddie

MOJO. i'm a cowboy today major

THE MAJOR (*swiping*). wasps – bastards

NARRATOR. mojo shot the wasps – bang bang bang – blatter blatter blatter

MOJO. is mickybo in mickybo's ma?

MICKYBO'S MA. he's not here

MICKYBO. yer a geg mickybo's ma – who has him – the spacemen or the gypos – tell us a story mickybo's ma – make us laugh

MICKYBO'S MA. tell ya a story – make ya laugh – i'm sittin here without a slice a bread – not a pot to piss in an the tv's shite – and mickybo's da the man that i love header an all that he is has lost the spark of life than once made him the man that he was – when's somebody gonna make me laugh – mickybo's in the entry kickin a ball

NARRATOR. nothing funny about that

MOJO. where'd ya get the ball mickybo?

MICKYBO. stole it – new one – go for the record – not today though

MOJO. me an ma ma's on holidays at ma auntie rita's – it's wick – she bleaches the floorboards an keeps pinchin my face – hate it

MICKYBO. wanna know what happened?

MOJO. aye

MICKYBO. it's bad like – it's not all bad like – it's like some bad some good an some very big

NARRATOR. the bad news

MICKYBO. gank the wank an fuckface burnt the hut an the rubber bullet with a petrolbomb they found up the entry

NARRATOR. the hut's gone – the good news

MICKYBO. i slit the tyres on fuckface's bike an built another hut – ya wanna see it it's weeker – no rubber bullet like but they'll be other riots – we'll get more

NARRATOR. the hut's back and rubber bullets are on their way – the bad news

MICKYBO. it wasn't fuckface's bike it was his older brother's torture – torture's a header – he pokes the eyes out a mad dogs an tells his ma to fuck up

NARRATOR. fuck up ma – the good news

MICKYBO. torture kicked the tubes out a fuckface cause i slit his tyres – an it had nothin to do with him

NARRATOR. torture – the very big news

MICKYBO. fuckface wants a fair dig between me an you an him an gank

MOJO. a fair dig with the both a them?

MICKYBO. i said no problem that we'd gliss the bake of the two a them

MOJO. they'll bury us

MICKYBO. yer from up the road – they wanna kick the tubes outta you anyway

NARRATOR. there's fights to be fought an battles to be won but before all that there's some slabberin to be done

MICKYBO. we'll fight ya fuckface at two o'clock up the entry – no witnesses just the four of us

FUCKFACE. no witnesses an no cryin to yer ma an da

MICKYBO. you'll be cryin fuckface – gonna kick the tubes outta ye

FUCKFACE. i'm gonna rip yer eyes out an stick them up yer arse

MICKYBO. up yer arse – shout somethin mojo

MOJO. up yer arse

MICKYBO. mojo's gonna kick gank up the balls an make them bleed – gank's balls are gonna bleed – big gank bloody balls

GANK. i'm gonna kick mojo's balls into the lagan an him after them

MICKYBO. two o'clock fuckface

FUCKFACE. smelly bastards

MICKYBO. you an yer ma's two smelly bastards

FUCKFACE. up yer hole

MICKYBO. up yer hole

MOJO. up yer hole

NARRATOR. up the entry – ring ring ding ding

MICKYBO. mojo get wired in

MOJO. you get wired in

FUCKFACE. lappers gank the two a them's lappers

GANK. lappers fuckface

MICKYBO. lapper that Fuckface

Mickybo hits Fuckface and they tussle with each other. Mojo shadow boxes and watches the fight.

mojo get wired in – kick gank up the balls

FUCKFACE. bury im gank

Gank and Mojo aren't keen. They make half-hearted attempts to go for each other. Fuckface is on top of Mickybo holding him down.

torture – torture – i have im – ambush – ambush

MOJO. barney rip the balls is in his yard – he's his big knife with him

Everything stops.

MICKYBO. fair dig over

FUCKFACE. torture – torture – ambush

Mickybo punches Fuckface. Mojo makes a half-hearted attempt to hit Gank then spits at him.

MICKYBO. mcmanus luigi riva

MOJO. riva riva

MICKYBO. run like fuck mojo

MOJO. run like fuck mickybo

NARRATOR. down the entry running like fuck over the timbers and into the hut

MICKYBO. ya think they saw us comin in?

MOJO. don't know

MICKYBO. did ya not look back?

MOJO. i just ran

MICKYBO. maybe the didn't chase us

MOJO. aye

MICKYBO. do ya think the chased us?

MOJO. yeah

MICKYBO. so do i – that ugly bastard bloodied my nose
(*Mickybo wipes his bloody nose with his sleeve.*) – did ya
get gank?

MOJO. kicked im up the balls four times an spat in his bake

MICKYBO. we did them – didn't we do them

MOJO. aye we did them

MICKYBO. do ya think barny rip the balls is with them?

MOJO. nah – what ya think?

MICKYBO. nah

MOJO. think they're out there waitin on us?

MICKYBO. aye – torture an rip the balls with em

MOJO. aye

MICKYBO. we'll get murdered

MOJO. murdered – you hadn't slit the bike we wouldn't be
gettin murdered

MICKYBO. they don't like you – we'd a got murdered anyway

MOJO. they don't like you too

MICKYBO. aye but they don't like you more than they don't
like me – they hate you – that's what they said – we hate
mojo

MOJO. i'm not fightin them again – the war's over – play in the park – better playin in the park

MICKYBO. after we get away we'll go to the park – if we were butch an sundance we could shoot our way out with real guns

MOJO. shoot the faces off em

MICKYBO. member the two a them sittin all shot up talkin about australia

MOJO. aye

MICKYBO. butch an sundance

MOJO. aye

MICKYBO. where we goin when we get out a here sundance

MOJO. the park

MICKYBO. no australia – butch an sundance are goin to australia

MOJO. shoot our way out

MICKYBO. run out the hut shootin an head for the bridge at the end of the timbers

MOJO. they get us they'll murder us

MICKYBO. they won't get us – they mightn't even be out there

MOJO. real guns be weeker

MICKYBO. aye – ya ready then

MOJO. right – one two three go

MOJO / MICKYBO. mcmanus luigi riva – don del a vista – flemanco – bingo – bang bang bang

They move from shooting to rolling down a hill.

MOJO. race ya up to the top again

MICKYBO. nah it's borin – butch an sundance didn't roll down hills

MOJO. the did when the bandits was after them

MICKYBO. it's borin – mon we'll get a bus an go to bolivia

NARRATOR. a bus to bolivia

MICKYBO. hay mister this bus go to bolivia?

BUSMAN. it does not – newcastle county down that's where this bus goes

MICKYBO. where's newcastle county down mister

BUSMAN. a long way from bolivia – i'd say it would be like bolivia though

MICKYBO. why haven't they burnt yer bus mister?

BUSMAN. i've a big stick here that's why – bate them good lookin

MICKYBO. we've no money mister – take us to newcastle county down – we're the men for newcastle county down

BUSMAN. no money is it – newcastle county down – it's the twelfth – one bus there one bus back – no pishin on the seats

MICKYBO. one bus there one bus back – no pishin on the seats

A bus to Bolivia.

BUSMAN. end of the road we're in bolivia

MICKYBO. right ya are mister

BUSMAN. and what would the lads be at in bolivia?

MICKYBO. we'll be at robbin banks an drinkin beer out a a bucket

BUSMAN. wise men yous are

MICKYBO. wise men mister an no pishin on the seats

BUSMAN. all the way to bolivia an no pishin on the seats

NARRATOR. bang bang bang bang – they shot the busman dead – then ran up a mountain – rolled down a hill – smelt all the cow shite – threw stones in the sea an pished over the rocks – marched in front of the parade

Narrator hums the Sash. Mickybo twirls a stick.

– then ran up the pier pretendin butch an sundance were bein chased by the posse

MICKYBO (*both hiding*). who are those guys?

MOJO. who are those guys?

MICKYBO. we can shoot or wait sundance

MOJO. we can't wait butch i'm starvin

MICKYBO. we'll shoot it out then

MOJO. they'll kill us

MICKYBO. mon we'll jump off the pier – they'll not follow us if we jump

As Butch and Sundance.

MOJO. no i want to fight it out

MICKYBO. we'll die

MOJO. we'll die if we jump

MICKYBO. we'll jump

MOJO. no

MICKYBO. why not?

MOJO. i'm not doin it

MICKYBO. don't be silly

MOJO. i just need one shot that's all

MICKYBO. why won't ya jump

MOJO. i can't swim

MICKYBO. can't ya swim really like?

MOJO. course i can – grab the stick

MICKYBO. one two three go

MOJO / MICKYBO. bang bang bang bang (*Jump off the pier.*) – oh shit

MICKYBO. alright mister we're goin home

BUSMAN. how'd the lads go in bolivia then – did yas rob banks an drink beer out of a bucket

MICKYBO. we played with the band an jumped into the water when the posse was chasin us just like butch an sundance did

BUSMAN. fine men yous are

MICKYBO. we are mister – we're fine men just like our das

BUSMAN. butch and sundance there's yas go

MICKYBO. from belfast to bolivia an back again mister

BUSMAN. from bolivia to belfast an back again an not a bank robbed

MICKYBO. good luck mister

BUSMAN. fine lads yous are

MICKYBO. fine lads we are

NARRATOR. butch an sundance makin a run for it to bolivia – two kids havin a geg – great lads – there was a crowd of people at the top of mickybo's street – blue flashin lights an screams you could hear forever – mickybo's ma held him tight – an all the while the sun shown down

MICKYBO (*pushes open saloon doors*). we were in newcastle county down today da – we pretended it was bolivia and we jumped into the sea

MICKYBO'S DA. newcastle is a fine place – me an yer ma used to go dancin there – newcastle is a fine place to go dancin

MICKYBO. we danced in front of the band da – it was a geg

MICKYBO'S DA. good man mickybo havin a geg

MICKYBO. are you dead da?

MICKYBO'S DA. i am that son – every square inch of me

MICKYBO. why da?

MICKYBO'S DA. i was sittin havin a pint thinkin about the world and all its glory an someone shot me – blew the back of my head clean off

MICKYBO. was it sore da?

MICKYBO'S DA. nah son it wasn't sore

MICKYBO. bet ya there was a lot a blood da – when yer shot there's a lot a blood isn't there da?

MICKYBO'S DA. any god's amount of it son

MICKYBO. if superman was there he would've stopped the bullet da wouldn't he

MICKYBO'S DA. aye son superman would've stopped the bullet

MICKYBO. does this mean we're not goin to australia da?

MICKYBO'S DA. i think it does son

MICKYBO. no gooday gooday gooday digger

MICKYBO'S DA. no gooday gooday gooday digger

MICKYBO. see ye then da

MICKYBO'S DA. good luck son

NARRATOR. that evenin mojo sat on the banks of the lagan an threw skimmers across the water – he threw until his arms were sore an there was nothin left to throw – then he made his way home – over the bridge and up the road – the road was empty but for the major still guardin the bonfire – even though there was nothin left to guard – mojo's da came to visit that night – he had a bunch of flowers an shiny shoes – mojo's ma smiled at the flowers but it didn't last long – soon the bullets started to fly – mojo slipped up to his bed – he lay and thought about mickybo an his da – night night sleep tight an don't let the bed bugs bite – after a few days he called for mickybo – blatter blatter blatter

MOJO. is mickybo in mickybo's ma?

MICKYBO'S MA. there's nobody here

MOJO. yer a geg mickybo's ma

MICKYBO'S MA. leave me alone an go away

NARRATOR. mojo mickybo – great lads – mickybo's in the hut along with gank an fuckface – they're smokin fegs an talkin the talk of men – it's showtime

FUCKFACE. wha do you want?

Silence.

MOJO. ya wanna go to the park an we'll roll down the hill

MICKYBO. nah – that's for kids – rollin down the hill's just for kids

FUCKFACE. where's mickybo's bike? – where's his bike? – me an gank saw ye ridin on his bike – didn't we see him ridin on mickybo's bike gank

GANK. we saw ye on mickybo's bike – where is it?

FUCKFACE. say to him mickybo

MICKYBO. i want ma bike back mojo – ya stole ma bike an i want it back – my da bought me that bike an i want it back

MOJO. i don't have yer bike mickybo – they stole it you said they stole it

GANK. he's callin you a liar fuckface

FUCKFACE. you calling me a liar – you an yer mates from up the road stole it

GANK. steal the bikes

MOJO. i don't have yer bike mickybo – i swear a don't have it – i'm yer mate

FUCKFACE. – he's mates with us now after what happened to his da – yer mates with us mickybo aren't ye

MICKYBO. aye – they saw ye on the bike – where's the bike mojo?

GANK. fight him mickybo

FUCKFACE. aye mickybo hit him

MOJO. i wanna go home

FUCKFACE. yer goin nowhere until ya fight mickybo – ya
said ya were gonna do it so do it mickybo

Mojo and Mickybo face each other.

MICKYBO. get me ma bike or i'll dig ya

MOJO. i don't have the bike mickybo you know i don't

MICKYBO. ya shouldn't have stole it – ya shouldn't have
fuckin stole it

Mickybo pulls Mojo to the ground and punches him.

MICKYBO. orange bastard – yas killed my da – ya dirty
fuckin orange bastard

NARRATOR. love many trust few and learn to paddle your
own canoe – years later i was walking through the town –
this town – belfast – a town with memories – i saw mickybo
across the street – mojo mickybo

MICKYBO. mickybo mojo

NARRATOR. we both pretended we didn't know each other
and walked on – mojo mickybo

In the hut.

MICKYBO. mickybo mojo

NARRATOR. what was the best day mickybo?

MICKYBO. best day what way mojo?

NARRATOR. best day best day ya tube

MICKYBO. there were loads of best days ya geek

NARRATOR. best day ever

MICKYBO. in the hut

NARRATOR. aye in the hut – it was weeker in the hut

MICKYBO. after we had the fight with gank the wank an fuckface

NARRATOR. aye

MICKYBO. they were all waitin outside the hut – the lot of them

NARRATOR. all waiting to kick the tubes out of us mickybo

MICKYBO. butch an sundance against the world

Narrator as a child from now on.

MOJO. where we going when we get outta here?

MICKYBO. butch an sundance are going to australia

MOJO. we'll shoot our way out

MICKYBO. run out the hut shootin an head for the bridge at the end of the timbers

MOJO. what happens if they get us

MICKYBO. they won't get us – they mightn't even be out there – be weeker if we had real guns

MOJO. aye – ya ready then?

MICKYBO. right

MOJO. one two three go

MOJO / MICKYBO. mcmanus luigi riva – bang bang bang bang bang bang

They freeze. As in the last scene of Butch Cassidy and the Sundance Kid *we hear a call to 'Fire', followed by a volley of rifle shots. Another volley of shots. Louder. The sound of the rifle shots becomes deafening.*

THE WAITING LIST

For Michael Brennan
my history teacher

The Waiting List was first performed at the Old Museum Arts Centre, Belfast, on 18 April 1994.

The play was performed by Lalor Roddy.

Directed by David Grant.
Produced by Point Fields Theatre Company.

*An empty stage except for the frame of a pram. The actor
should be in his mid-thirties and wearing either a dressing
gown or pyjamas.*

a big sherman tank of a pram jammed against the front door –
prams to keep children in and bad boys out – they have a list –
a shopping list for taigs fenians popeheads pan-nationalists
republicans catholics – not two hundred yards and two weeks
away this fella's in the sack with his girlfriend

night night dear
night night dear

door kicked in – bang bang bang bang – end of story

now there's a list – and you never know i might be a desirable
commodity – on sales as it were – lingering in the bargain
basement so to speak – i'd rather be past my sell by date but
i'm not even half way to my allotted three score and ten – plus
i'm not working at the moment which means your waiting
time's doubled or seems like it cause i've nothing to do except
paint the house a shitty yellow colour and push the youngsters
– in the sherman tank – through this mixed – but not
completely integrated area – mixed only in the sense that i
couldn't put a flag out or douse petrol over mountains of wood
in the middle of the street and get a spark from two flints to
make it whoosh – singing fuck this and fuck that – while
scribbling down misspelt names on the back of a feg box with
a well chewed biro stolen from the bookies – mixed in that
sense – not that i'd ever want to do those things you
understand but you never know – that's the problem round here
you never know – a wee bit of fear keeps you on your toes –
never quite at ease – just slightly edgy – i could always ask i
suppose – next time i'm doing the shopping and i see one of
the lads poncing round dunnes stores with his dark glasses pot
belly chunky gold jewellery fat wife and snattery children

excuse me am i on your list? – in between everything you need
for a ulster fry in one pack and a slimy bag of frozen chips –
five per cent less fat of course – i would like to know – it would
help me in my capacity as decision maker if i knew i was
going to be around to view the consequences of my decisions

it's hard to say kid
he whispers out the side of his mouth while – one of his
snattery skinhead kids claws at his ma's taut bulging mini skirt
for a toy machine gun – (they learn early) – with real imitation
bullets flashing lights and noises just like the one rambo has
sewn in between his muscular thighs – as he beats a track
through the jungle blasting the shit out of the dirty gooks

it's open season you see kid – it's difficult to tell – it's a lottery
your number's in the hat what more can i say – after the
shopping i always give her one on the sofa – do you wanna
watch?

so i'm waiting here – night after night – pram against the door
– looking across the street to the house i was brought up in –
thinking – musing – playing with the idea – why would it be
me? – am i on the list?

tock tick tock tick tock tick – football in the entry – twenty
aside – dogshit everywhere – use it for goal posts – i'm
geordie best – dribble dribble swerve faint swerve dribble
dribble – looks up – (sign of a good player always looks up) –
whack – and it rattles the net – the crowd go mad – geordie
geordie geordie – united thirty-seven chelsea sixteen – stick
insects sliding in the shit and dreaming of wembley – (not
croke park)

goal
off side
your ma
aye your ma

dawn to dusk – a big boy appears on the scene – hair down to
his arse jeans up to his arse and boots gleaming – shined by his
loving mother four times a day

he's a scout sent by matt busby i've seen him in the park

the stick insects gather round – ears pricked – eyes like saucers
– minds agog

are you a scout?
aye sort of – (ha ha ha) – you you and you

whisper whisper

my da told me some guy gets over a hundred quid a week and
he only plays for spurs
jesus
bollocks
what'd he say?
who you playing for?
will your ma let you go?
fuck up fenian bastard

smack smack kick kick – a bloody nose and me geordie best
too – football jerseys off tartan scarves on – mcdonald
mcdougall mcclaymore mckingbilly the clan of robbie burns –
who gives a fuck – and me i'm still geordie boy and sure a
good kicking never does you any harm anyway – demarcation
lines are drawn – whatever they are

don't go here don't go there watch who you play with be in
before dark

father
the boy should take up boxing – good clean sport – discipline
the mind – defend yourself
mother
it'll ruin his good looks – look at your fid you ugly wee bugger

high cheek bones – i should have been a movie star but was
never spotted – not by anyone from hollywood anyway – just
keep playing and it'll all go away that's the trick – failed the
quallie that year – couldn't believe it – einstein i was – got
a bike for being a failure – a gobi desert summer – ulster 71
in full swing – dodgems helter skelter waltzers big wheel – a
quick thrill to unite the warring tribes – i'm on my bike –
peddle peddle peddle – everywhere everyday – after wembley
that big race in france was getting a turn – three of us this day
– a biking gang – the ton-up boys – get lost and end up in
some – get a damp cockroach infested flat on the nineteenth

floor for your demob suit estate – not like the entry – no dog
shit anywhere – a bit of greenery and a playground – swings
see-saw roundabout climbing frame – all good stuff – the ton-
up boys

where you from?
what school do you go to?
what football team do you support?
say the alphabet
sing the sash

should have taken up boxing looks as if the cheek bones are
going to get a burl anyway
push faster faster faster – faster you fenian bastard – need a
rest sit on the grass – feel your mate's dick

smack

feel it you fruity fucker – this one's a fruit and a fenian

punch – dr martens – kick kick kick – children can be cruel
bastards they're like adults that way – i'm starting to get the
hang of this now – i'm a taig and they're orangemen – what
could be simpler – things are starting to hot up – houses and
petrol bombs – hand in hand – made for each other – there's
nothing like a bit of heat on a cold night when you're watching
crossroads – the place was never the same after sandy bit the
dust – that's what brought meg's bad headaches on you know –
a mate of mine left his dog to guard the house – whoof – the
orangemen called him hot-dog – made him crazy – nothing
like a bit of humour – the parish priest after having a yarn with
the almighty formed a stop dogs going whoof in the dark of
night vigilante group – patrolling the streets with hurls and bin
lids – all dogs can sleep save in their kennels – it's their
owners who do the tossing and turning – myself i'm doing a
bit more of the former than the latter

there's a wee girl fancies you two streets away – she's a
protestant
what do you think lads?
get in there you're a cert thing
all orangewomen do it
do you see the diddies on her she didn't get them sitting by the
fire

seven o'clock next night up the entry – find a patch with no
patch shit – (ha ha) – talk talk talk – lumber lumber lumber –
feelie feelie feelie

let's do this on a regular basis
why not you're such a nice guy

floating on air – tiptoeing from cloud to cloud – i'm in love –
i'm in lust – i'm in deep shit – next day skipping down the
corridors of knowledge pulled – three hard men – the ra –
boy's version – shiny oxfords bald heads earrings short
parallels black socks – the uniform

we've been told you're seeing an orangewoman – please
refrain from this anti-social activity
but you don't understand men – (men?) – feelie feelie the
diddies and the bliff

smack – just to clear the wax from my ears

her brother's inside for murder – put your country before your
dick or we'll beat the shit out of you

silence silence silence – lumber lumber lumber – feelie feelie
feelie – it's all over-flow as the plumber said to his girl

why?
i'm frightened
oh
well men how'd i do? – the republican cause will never die
while i'm alive sure it won't

blah blah blah – school – halcyon days

homework boy late boy hair boy earring boy cursing boy

blackboard compass – whack whack whack – the inside of a
tractor tyre cut to shape – whack whack whack – best years of
your life – there was one guy though – history teacher –
always talking about sun yat-sen and his wee merry men –
community worker hands across the divide type – big
moustache no tie long hair cord jacket desert boots – a hip guy
– he took a shine to me – used to tell me dirty jokes and let me
smoke in the store room – me and him him and me – brought
me to the youth club – got me interested in table tennis – he

used to bring me home when the tartans were on the hunt –
sun yat-sen and his wee merry men – i'm standing in the gym
this night – not half a brick's throw away from the table tennis
room – watching fellas with low cheekbones beat the shit out
of each other – bang bang bang bang – you see there was a
pane of glass missing from one of the windows in the table
tennis room – and if you had a mind to – if you put yourself
out a bit you could have climbed over the front wall crawled
through the long grass on your elbows and knees like a
commando aimed a gun through the missing pane and . . . – if
you had a mind to – a hole in the head – thick purple blood on
a cord jacket – a smart man with brains hanging out of him –
the anti had just been upped – men steal lives while boys play
games – skip teak stick ra hey man no prob

let's join up
i will if you will

ten pence a week – funds – football teams written in a black
book – all code you know – i'm arsenal – the gunners – (ha ha
ha) – no readies forthcoming and it's smack smack smack –
even revolutionaries must think in commercial terms –
education officer that's me – lectures in someone's da's garage
that smelt of car oil and home brew – padraig pearce wolfe
tone robert emmet henry joy mccracken – matinee and evening
performances all repeated – i'm not into research

who didn't pay their divvies this week? – goody goody

stage one – this is a gun this is how you clean a gun this is
how you hold a gun this is how you hide a gun – stage two –
when being chased while carrying a gun fall to the ground roll
head over heels or arse over bollocks stand upright and
confront the enemy – stage three – scout uniforms and drill –
march march march left right left right turn left turn right
attention at ease fart belch spit scratch your nuts – all in irish –
big day – march down some street in some area to
commemorate some guy who was murdered some time ago –
baden powell gear on a pair of shades and away we go – up
and down and down and up up and down and down and up –
what a boyo i am – is this worth the price of four singles a
week or what – can yous all see me – up and down and down

and up and away we go – la la la la la . . . – spotted – informed
on – someone out of my da's work – shout shout shout – bawl
bawl bawl – clip round the ear – one less volunteer in the
struggle for freedom

i want to leave
you'll have to get a kicking
don't worry i'm getting used to it

took up gaelic football after that – a bit of culture in the
sporting arena

and it's colm mcalarney over the bar

agricultural sports – it's a game for close knit communities
who breathe fresh air and there's me alienated and likes the
smell of petrol fumes – maybe i just didn't have the bottle for
it – i was walking down the road one night after training when
i was pulled by the – why don't you go out and catch some
terrorists mob

who are you? – where you coming from? – where you going
to? – how do you spell your name?

all the time spread-eagled – normal practice – the boys are full
of jungle juice – laughing and joking – rifle barrel in the
middle of my back

why don't you play soccer you fucker – republican fucking
sport – we know where you live you bastard

still laughing as i ran home – fuck this for a game of darts –
have to get out of here find myself – the big old u s of a is the
place for that – bring a dram of irish whiskey and a piece of
linen in case you bump into an old sod for the old sod – i met
this thirty stone homosexual drug pusher – ate everything from
a bag of coal to a hamburger – just like the movies it was –
heat wave old folk in dallas dropping like flies and there's
tomatoes the size of your fist – wake up go to the beach
worship the sun god get stoned eat fist like tomatoes get stoned
couple of beers get stoned go to bed – bliss – ireland never
heard of the place

you've a lovely voice – your vocal patterns are so lyrical – it
sounds like you're singing all the time it's really beautiful –

fuck up and pass the joint
have a shot – all harps drink whiskey – god bless the ole sod –
four green fields

all crying their lamps out

the british are mother fuckers – protestants are mother fuckers
– niggers yids pollacks spicks wops chinks gooks ruskies and
those no good low down bastards who kicked custer's ass – all
mother fuckers – i'd love to see the place – my granny's from
leeson street do you know that – a civil war – jees that must be
great – do you have fish in ireland?

eyes opened – mind broadened – time to go

say hi to your folks – have a nice journey man

i travelled – i broke free – now i'm an enlightened person
unaffected by my hideous surroundings – i am above the
humdrum – aloft and aloof – education – back to school –
grind grind grind – swot swot swot – university – philosophy –
a higher plane – socrates plato aristotle heidigger sartre
epistemology phemanonology metaphysics logic – nationalists
loyalists – bollocks – communists – shoulder to shoulder with
your fellow man or woman – sorry person – human – sweat of
the brow – the common good – solicitors digging holes binmen
performing heart surgery that's the business – invited to a
meeting i was – oh aye – walked into this bar hole in my jacket
to look the part – full of ole lads society didn't give a toss
about and the place reeked of piss brilliant

no i'm afraid we're upstairs

a log fire woolly jumpers beards and pints of guinness –
everyone babbling about the mating habits of wood pigeons
and obscure french film directors in between giving the
capitalist lackies a verbal pasting

when i was younger my history teacher was shot dead – why
do things like that happen?
after mating the male sits on the eggs – wood pigeons share
their parental responsibilities – wood pigeons have a lot to
teach us if only we would listen
why don't we move downstairs it's a bit too cosy up here

i think we're just fine here – you can enlighten them without
mixing with them – god you're so naïve

and some guy in the corner wearing a save whale sperm t-shirt
picks his horses from the guardian and rips a hole in his new
denims – on the jukebox they're playing – give peace a chance
– give my friggin head peace – i never went back – not that i
was missed – wood pigeons were never my thing

then i met a girl – by chance – at a dance – not that i ever do –
unless i'm drunk and then i can't

i love you
i love you too

ding dong ding dong – wedding bells – went to spain for our
honeymoon – all sun sand and sangria – just like the brochure
said – met up with this crowd from – belfast

it's great to be away
why can't belfast be like this?
i've no problems loving my neighbour
why can't we live together?

reaching for my second crate of san miguel and reflecting on
the moral decline of the western world i said

it seems to me or shall i say it is my considered opinion that
communism – on paper at least – is indeed the best system
under which humans can live
commie bastard

you can't win can you – holidays out children in – it's time to
settle down – philosopher's don't earn much readies – it's
understandable there's no real need for it in these parts – then
someone says to me – you look like a tiler – and i thought
maybe i do – mix a bucket of stuff fire it on the floor fire it on
the wall get the tiles slap them on grout it all up and there you
go – bathrooms kitchens and the odd en suite – life couldn't be
better – there's a bit of money coming in the kids have new
uniforms and i'm too old to be chased – i'm thinking this place
isn't so bad so long as you stick to a routine – (which you
can't really help doing cause that's the way things are) – and
ignore everything around you (which is what we all do

anyway) – happy days – i even brought the kids down to see
the tall ships – i mean to say – it's like you can be here and not
really live here – you look but don't see – you hear but don't
listen – and you think but don't question – it's great – then my
slumber is interrupted – i'm standing in a bathroom this day
slapping on some nearly expensive wouldn't have them in my
own house pink tiles – i broke about four of them on the trot –
(had to get rid of them quick in case i was sued for negligence)
– semi-detached car caravan motor bike two children and a
good looking wife – (i lingered on her for a while it must be
the seven year itch) – who doesn't need to work – this guy
worked in mackies and when things were going bad shifted
and earned his crust in shorts – mobility – good if you can get
it – the job's finished – everyone's happy – a cup of tea put
some paper on the sofa before you sit and some chocolate
bickies

will you take a cheque?
certainly we're here to accommodate you the customer

his writing was like my wee lad's and he couldn't spell my
name – now here's me sometimes working sometimes not
sometimes money sometimes potless – and there's him flitting
from place to place gathering a pile of goodies on the way –
sure it's not his fault – if you've a seat reserved on the gravy
train you're hardly going to hang around the station are you –
why don't i ever cop on – you see whenever i'm pushing the
kids round these streets in the sherman tank i keep thinking to
myself – this is where i've lived all my life – this is my
community – but it's not – i don't feel at ease here – my whole
life hemmed in – jesus what a waste

and now there's a list

I WON'T DANCE – DON'T ASK ME

For all those who ever shouted
'Lift them Pinky'

I Won't Dance – Don't Ask Me was first performed at the Ulster Arts Club, Belfast, on 15 November 1993.

The role of Gus McMahon was played by Sean Caffrey, who also directed.

Produced by Who The Hell Theatre Company.

This production subsequently toured throughout Ireland.

Empty stage but for armchair. It's four o'clock in the morning.
Gus McMahon can't sleep. He is in the living room of his
house with his cat Sparky. Gus is drinking a bottle of
Guinness. His wife and son are both asleep upstairs.

are you listening sleepers? – fuck you and the wallpaper –
wallpaper my fuck – sparky cat – having a sleep pets – did the
wallpaper trick disturb you pets? – livers? – does my sparky
pet want some livers? – livers for my pets – you must let them
know sparky – make them listen

she thought i'd balls it up you see – i would but that's not the
point – she's working i'm not – she papers the room – that
makes me look bad – she wasn't thinking when people aren't
thinking you must let them know remember that sparky – the
old thought trick – people don't think then they listen to other
people who don't think – that's what's wrong no thinking – we
know sparky don't we – think

the boy doesn't think – the boy – the sample – always have
more than one – alone too often you see it affects their mind –
i'm standing in the kitchen pouring soup into a pot – guinness
and oyster good stuff – i put a drop of water in the tin and fire
it into the pot – you shouldn't do that – he says – the soup's
ready as it is – do you understand that sparky do you
understand a mind that works like that? – it's my soup if i
wanted to have a lilian gish in the pot it's up to me isn't it –
you know what he does though – he puts the tops back on
empty milk bottles then puts them back in the fridge – who in
their right fucking mind does that? – he says to me there's no
god the world's made up solely of atoms and that my
generation are emotionally retarded and he puts the tops back
on empty fucking milk bottles – those wee silver chats you just
throw them away – if there's an empty milk bottle in your

fridge you tell it to get out to fuck and make way for the full
chats – then what would i know

are you the only one that listens to me sparky? – this morning
– that's it – this morning – the three of us were sitting round
the breakfast table this morning – bread butter jam toast
cornflakes tea coffee orange juice – bliss – she was dressed for
work – blue suit important looking – and the boy was waiting
on his lift to college dressed like an out of work poet – maybe
we could meet for lunch in town my treat – yeah i've only one
lecture this afternoon metaphysics and its analysis yeah about
half one – make it earlier i've a meeting with my head of
department at two – is there any milk left? – (must remember
to buy some) – nothing – i've nothing worth saying so they
don't listen – bye gus – i'm here i'm sitting at the table – bye
bye bye – don't forget the milk – vanished – time to go – i'm
alone – i just sat there couldn't move didn't want to move –
stuck rigid – i'm stirring at the tea pot too long – it goes
blurred then everything in the room's up close to me – close
my eyes drifting off – then i saw a mountain and i was
standing at the bottom of it and it was raining round balls of
rain – perfect round balls – and i had no coat on – what the
fuck's happening to me? – the boy thinks i drink too much –
what do you reckon sparky? – he doesn't know what he's
talking about he doesn't know the story – it's about who i am –
what i did – he thinks it's enough to call me gus – i know who
you are because we're on first name terms – no there's more to
it than that – drink and the betting game go hand in hand –
bacon and eggs brandy and a good cigar – when i started up
i had a choice learn from those who know or become a pencil
stealer a clock watcher a nine to five – i obey the rules yes sir
i do – you see those people are small petty minded dishonest
tosspots hiding behind whatever rule regulation document
decision fucking lie they're told to – it was like that then and
it's the same now – it's all logos value for money computer
print outs nice spongy black sofas – what about people nobody
thinks in terms of people anymore – it's all a million miles an
hour – no time – no time just eat lunch at your desk – i always
wanted to stay clear of that you see – have a drink get to know
people make the whole thing social give it a meaning – fuck

what time it is make this part of your life not just a job –
there's no sense to it then – drink was all part of that – race
meetings the dogs clerking for some fella who'd pay you over
the odds if he won – point to points coarsing – whatever it
was – just make it more than pay cheques and stealing fucking
pencils – it was personal to me that's the whole thing it was
personal

how do you explain that to them when they're sitting down to
lunch talking about department meetings and metaphysics –
how do you do that? – lunch – i was overlooked on that one –
i don't eat lunch anymore sparky do you know that – i haven't
earned it so i can't eat it – lunch is for workers people who
work eat lunch and i don't work – i don't work – sure don't
you look after the house gus – that's it – i'm fifty-four and i
look after the house – that's it – dusting shelves scraping pots
and folding sheets – i must be the fucking envy of the western
world – what an idyllic little life – that can't be what i end up
with – it isn't right – it's not fair – when she comes home from
work what have i got to tell her – of what importance is it?

did you have a nice day – yes so did i – any post? – a letter
from the book club – chops for dinner? – chops for dinner –
oh by the way after you left this morning i drank a few bottles
of guinness and read the obituaries – did you know our
milkman's sister died in a car crash – it's awful sad she left
three young children behind and a husband who's an alcoholic
– not that makes him a bad person you understand – oh i forgot
to tell you the grocer's doing a special on watermelons this
week so i bought thirty-six fucking dozen just in case – i left
some of those nice chocolate biscuits you like in the cupboard

what type of thoughts are they to fill your head with? – and
then the boy says – why don't you read some jean paul sartre
enlighten yourself – that's a bit of a fucking leap sparky isn't it
– chocolate bickies and watermelons to jean paul sartre –
enlighten my mind – jesus – oh i'm enlightened alright – the
boy's getting married soon right – right – he's still a student –
not a pot to piss in but that's his business – thirty years i've
been married – does he ask me anything – no – i know – if
i know he must know that's my responsibility – it's a duty –

my duty – you won't get this from a book boy – always
carrying books end up with arms like one of those pink arsed
monkey chats – what do you reckon about this marriage trick –
have you given it any thought what do you reckon? – it'll be
alright – what do you really know about it? – nothing i haven't
been married yet – do you want to know what it's all about i'll
tell you will i – i'll do that for you – have you ever seen your
girlfriend go to the toilet – no – well that's what marriage is all
about – blank face – i'm trying to tell you something here
listen – and then he's away

romantic notions – it's my job to get rid of those sparky – it's
not right to think like that – you marry a person not an image –
it's important to know that so i told him – if jean paul sartre or
plato or one of those other head up the metropole people had
have told him that – no but because it was me – i just didn't
want him to look at her one day and realise he didn't know her
– all that time wasted it's no good

reality sparky not myths – robert redford should have been a
bastard with bad teeth that would have sorted all this out –
he should have beat the cleevers out of his wife whored about
and generally fucked things up – that would have destroyed
the image – made things easier for everyone – a picture of
jane fonda – first thing in the morning boking her ring up after
being out on the piss all night that's what we want – but no –
a touch of romance a quick bit of the old cough rock and life
will be hunky dorry for ever and a day – the yanks have it all
sussed movieland that's where we live – the world's one big
m.g.m fucking studio – the world's your oyster bigger is better
look after yourself happy ending – that's how i lost my job you
know the bigger is better conspiracy has filtered down –
expansion is the way forward it's the only answer and if you
don't like it hasta la viste baby

twenty years i managed that bookies then bang it's sold – too
small need to expand – new staff all young – bright eyed bushy
tailed shiny hair and floppy suits – thank you here's a framed
photocopy of a print of some horse called arkle – mind the step
on your way out – that'll not happen to robert redford will it? –
what does my wife say sparky – what little pearl of wisdom

does she come off with – sure you need the rest gus you've
been working all your life take it easy – that's when i knew –
once she uttered those words i knew – you don't know who
i am do you – i'm a worker – that's all i do i don't know
anything else – why do you think i can't hang fucking
wallpaper

when i worked sparky – when i worked i was in control – i had
a place in this world and it was inside that betting shop – i was
an artist – i used to write up a meeting on the blackboard and
stand back and just stare at it and all the time i was thinking
christ i'm good there's no one does that better than me – it
wasn't much but i was the best – it was like looking in a mirror
i could see myself in my own handwriting – i looked at it
i recognised it and i knew it was me – that's been taken away
from me do you understand what i'm saying sparky it's gone –
i turned my back and some person who wants to make their
mark in the world because they've been told that's the right
thing to do makes a decision about my life – someone who
doesn't know me made a decision about my life – that's not
right – decisions behind closed doors – that's where we're at –
whisper whisper and keep that door shut – all doors must be
shut – they're on the inside you're on the outside

i went back today sparky – went back – i needed to see some
familiar faces – slap on the back the place isn't the same
without you gus – i don't know why i wanted that maybe it
was that thing at the breakfast table – the old round balls of
rain trick sparky – we always want to go back – the past's
there inviting us to dance and just as you've finished putting
your top hat and tails on the music stops – it's all in the head
sparky pets – the past's all in the napper

i walked straight in through the door and nothing – i didn't
recognise anything – it used to be a small place no bigger than
this room – the punters all huddled together – there were
blackboards on two of the walls and the other two were
covered in newspapers – the place was always littered with
dockets nearly every inch of the floor and in the background
the radio'd be blurting out the commentary – newmarket
chepstow uttoxeter kelso doncaster the curragh – the one fifty

five at newmarket seven furlongs the going's good to soft –
they're at the six furlong marker – brave boy and our rita
followed by parliament piece – brave boy and our rita – brave
boy – come on my son lift them pinkie – i turned to look at the
boards compare the writing you know but they weren't there –
just tv screens about ten of them – each one had the runners of
a race on them then the word off would flash up and when the
race was over the screen would change and the result would
appear – no horses no jockeys no race just words – this was a
lifeless place with no soul – i looked around for faces i knew
and spotted one so i walked over to him – did you get the last
winner – nah i backed the second co – then he turned away and
got on with the business of picking his next loser – i used to
have a gargle with this man – when he was short of a few quid
i'd let him have a bet and he'd pay me at the weekend – i knew
him and now he didn't know how to talk to me – he had things
to do sparky pets his own life to lead – i wasn't part of that
anymore – do you understand that i was of no use to him so he
didn't want to know – he didn't want to know

then it happened again – everybody was moving it felt like
they were all coming towards me – their mouths opening and
closing but no noise – i'm here look at me i'm here – the
words inside my head i kept thinking i have to get them out –
they can't stay there forever i have to get them out – i closed
my eyes – i felt everyone moving around me – it's all blurred
and spinning spinning – i can't move legs like lead weights –
i'm beginning to sweat – i'm here i'm fucking here can't you
see me – everything stopped – no action just like the tv
screens – standing rigid – are you alright son – some old man
in front of me – a big red face right up close – must leave must
leave now – then i was back in the street and it was over – if i
was to tell that to the boy he'd explain it in molecules and
chemical reactions – fuck that – have you finished your livers
sparky pets – that's it you give yourself a good wash

i'm not going mad i'm not there is just some things i don't
understand – can you be married for thirty years and not know
if you love the woman you're married to – then there's the boy
– i told him he was incapable of loving someone – i think
you're incapable of loving someone i said – jesus – he just

kept staring at me – i could see it in his face – why do you
want to hurt me – that's what he was thinking – and i was
thinking because you're my son – i'm angry and i need to cut
someone and you're the only one left – you're on the way up
and i'm on the way down and sometimes that's difficult to take
– there were no words after that – i should've explained to him
but i didn't – it's me – do you hear that it's me not you –
there's something happening here and i don't know what it is –
but it's me not you – you see sparky – i can't explain things –
to people – to him – i never could

when the boy was about twelve he was playing a football
match it was the first time he was picked for the school team –
it was important – i wanted to be there – this was my chance to
be there for him – i was always busy with work and that you
know not that i was one of those ambitious pushy types it's just
what i did – his mother bought him new boots he didn't want
them – embarrassed in front of his mates i suppose but she
insisted – he was full of energy chasing everything running
himself into the ground eager to do well – maybe just having
fun – that's it son you show them take no prisoners kid – him
and another boy were running for the ball – head on towards
each other – go on boy you can do it go on go on – just at the
last second he pulled away from the tackle he was taken off
after that – i followed him into the dressing room – he was
sitting on a bench looking at the new boots the ones he didn't
want in case he didn't play well and then the rest of the team
would all say to him – why'd your ma buy you boots when you
can't play football – do you know what i said to him sparky do
you know what i said – nice pair of boots – no pat on the back
and hard luck kid no there'll be other matches son don't worry
– nice pair of boots – you have to learn to talk to people it
doesn't come natural you got to work at it – i was too busy
then and now i don't know how – so it's all no water in the
soup and tops on empty fucking milk bottles

do you know what i think sparky pets i think there's something
in the water that's making us all go ga ga – that's what
happens you know no sweat about it – are you thirsty take that
wee cup of water – and all of a sudden the head's gone –

do you know anyone that's wise? – no – everyone's napper's
gone – you think you have one you're talking away to someone
and you think this is it here we are the only sane person i know
– and then you realise they're wearing slip-ons and white socks
– and then you take another look and the trousers are too short
or the head starts twitching or they start smelling their food
and then you think hold on here what's going on – in a couple
of years' time we'll all be sitting in front of the tv gulping
down pints of water while waiting for the special fried rice to
be delivered – there'll be no need to go outside the house just
plug your computer into the tv do your work then order
whatever clothes or food you need – everybody will be selling
something one big market place – that'll be their job – every
product will be multi purpose – inflatable rubber tea towels
you can use as picture frames and if taken short wipe your arse
with – briefcases you fold inside out and use as deep sea
diving suits – i flicked the tv on the other day sparky and this
happy woman of about fifty with teeth like a snow blizzard
who had just climbed the south face of k2 barefoot or crossed
the atlantic in a shoe box or something was telling me this new
shampoo would do wonders for my hair – it had a dye in it that
was the natural colour of your hair but better – better? – what
the fuck does that mean – it's not better it's just different that's
all – and then some poor bugger's sitting by their electric fire
which only has one bar on because they're skint – watching
this and thinking i wonder should i improve the gingerness of
my hair – so they buy it use it and stand in front of the mirror
and think – yes – i am complete – i am ready for the world
today and is my hair ginger or what – my life's going to
change i know it let's go – it's a lie they're being told a lie
nothing's going to change – in another ten minutes that one
bar's going to go out and they're going to be freezing the rest
of the day – no k2 no atlantic ocean no excitement just
different colour hair and a cold house

i've gone the other way now sparky pets i can't believe
anything – i can't read the newspaper can't watch television –
i've stopped listening to people i don't know and those i do
know i only half listen to – it wasn't meant to be like this –
this wasn't the picture i had – i always thought that things

would be clearer the older i got but they're not – i can't make
decisions anymore – today i was standing in the bakery –
gravy rings 23p for one or five for 99p jam doughnuts 29p for
one or four for 99p – i shouldn't know that i'm fifty-four and i
know the price of gravy rings and jam doughnuts – how many
men my age know the price of those things – i should be in
work where i belong – i'm standing at the counter it's my turn
and the woman's looking at me pissed off because she put her
washing out this morning before she came to work and now
it's belting down and she's going to have to do it all again and
no one's going to thank her for it

what do you want?
i don't know
this is a bakery
a jam doughnut no a gravy ring
what do you normally get?
i alternate today's gravy ring day
a gravy ring then
why not a jam doughnut?
i don't know
neither do i

i used to be responsible for the running of a business and now i
can't decide between two friggin buns – i tried to tell her about
the doughnut thing but it was no use – she didn't understand
what i was talking about what i was saying – you know what
she said to me sparky she said – why didn't you buy currant
squares? – i don't like currant squares we've been married
thirty years and she doesn't know i don't like currant squares –
i don't like them – i thought you did – when have you ever
seem me eat one? – i can't remember – before we were
married we were in your house in the parlour your mother
came in with tea and currant squares – would you like a
currant square gus? – no thank you i don't like them – can't
you remember it isn't that long ago? – i've a report to fill in
gus can we discuss this later – you see she has more important
things to think about that's why she can't remember – but me
i've plenty of time so i remember everything every useless
unimportant stupid detail – would you like a currant square

gus – no thank you i don't like them – i don't want to
remember things like that that isn't what i want in my head –
they just appear rattling around in there

when i was sixteen i went to the pictures to see the ladykillers –
alec guinness and peter sellers were in it – i sat on some
chewing gum and it ruined my good trousers – what's the point
in knowing that – what's it doing there? – if i'd have been in
work and that thought had flashed by i'd have said get to fuck
out i've other things to do people are depending on me – row f
third seat over from the centre – two rows ahead directly in front
of me was a man and women in their mid-forties they talked
the whole way through the picture – at the interval i bought an
ice cream and a bag of lemon bon bons – alec guinness played
the head of a gang of bank robbers – his landlady found out so
they tried to kill her but all their attempts back-fired – when
i left the cinema it was raining – so what?

alec guinness? – jesus – never liked him he can act none –
arthur guinness that's my man – a bottle of guinness and a
johnny walker black nothing else – that's how you break the
back of it – don't change your drink always stick to the same
gear and your swanny river will stay the course and distance –
and no smoking – i keep telling people cut the oily regs out
they're no good – a killer – you must look after yourself – i
can still do press ups sparky did you know that – oh yes and
the correct way too none of this starting off laying down
business – stand straight arms out in front of you drop to the
floor and right into them

*He does this collapsing when he hits the floor. He stays
there out of breath.*

i used to be able to do it but you didn't know me then sparky

*He sits up, puts his legs straight out and tries to touch his
toes. Fails. He feels a sharp pain in his back.*

jesus christ – pain's good for the soul sparky pets – good for
the soul

He crawls to the chair and pulls himself onto it.

it is my fuck

Silence.

do cats get prostrate problems – do they sparky? – have you
started to piss in instalments – i can't sleep anymore because
i keep thinking i'm going to wet the bed – i dose off about five
in the morning then i'm up again at seven – work time – i was
always an early riser – the other night i fired a lot of guinness
and benylin into me – knock me out – i wet the bed – after
fifty-four years i'm starting to piss the bed – she didn't say
anything – i admire her for that she could've made a big deal
out of it – maybe she was thinking i'm married to an animal
who soaks our bed with his own piss – she didn't say it though
– i spent the whole day with the mattress propped against the
wall and the hair dryer on – just tighten the muscles in your
buttocks when you're urinating mr mcmahon – thank you
doctor – brilliant now i'm going to end up with an arse as tight
as a pinhole – i'm frightened sparky – that frightens me – no

*He takes a small bottle of smelling salts from his pocket and
sniffs it in.*

the old smelling salts trick – keep the head right – ballroom
dancing – the good old ballroom dancing that's the business –
what do you know sparky about the old one two three one two
three – why don't we take a night class in ballroom dancing
gus? – very perceptive my wife – she sees there's something
not quite right and being the good lady she is wants to help – a
bolt of lightening a stroke of genius ballroom fucking dancing

i used to be a pretty good mover too – jiving that was my thing –
now her thing you see is night classes – anything and everything
advancing her mind slowly by degrees – a computer class here
a flower arranging class there yoga tank maintenance build
your own house – she made that pretty little vase over there –
now i couldn't do that that's not my bag as they say – she
also mentioned swimming and driving but only in passing –
maybe she thought they were a bit too advanced for me at the

moment – i know i know what you're thinking i should do
these things keep myself active join in – but you see sparky –
i thought i could get through life avoiding them that's what
i had prepared myself for – but i've been caught – a spotlight is
glaring down on me and picking me out as a waster because
all the others thrown on the shit heap – redundancy paid off
business bust or whatever they're all swimming and driving in
their droves – people who fainted in the bath or couldn't sit
in the back of a taxi without spewing are now all johnny
weismuller and graham fucking hill – all these things are
starting to build up now you see – i can't hang wallpaper i can't
swim i can't drive and i won't learn to waltz – where would i
drive to? – where would i swim to? – where would i waltz to?

i never wanted to swim – if i had've i would've that hasn't
changed – would i be cured doing length after length after
meaningless length? – no – then fuck it – would it make me
any more productive in the world? – no – then fuck it – would
i gain people's respect by swimming? – no – but it's not even
that you see sparky – if i start doing those things it means i've
given in i'll have accepted that i'm no longer of any use in the
real world so i'll spend my time waltzing and swimming –
and maybe i'll combine the two and go for that synchronised
bollocks – no not me not yet not ever – not gus mcmahon –
no – they won't do that to me – i won't be forced to spend my
life doing things i never wanted to do – i don't want to make a
vase and she can't make me – do you hear that? – no vases –
no wallpaper and no fucking vases

ballroom dancing – i think they should put it on the national
health sparky pets – next please – what's wrong with you off
the rocker is it – i've booked you in for five sessions down at
the plaza that'll sort you out – having problems with your
bladder i've just the thing – nurse the jitter bug music –
everything's geared towards making you feel worthless – a
burden – i had to make an appointment to sign on and then i
was referred to as one of their clients – do you want to work
mr mcmahon? – i'd prefer to go on a world cruise but with
readies being tight and that – maybe that's something you
could sort out for me – you're at a difficult age you understand
you have valuable hands on experience – it's a pity you

weren't ten years younger – i'm sorry i can't help you it's this
ageing process thing i can't seem to be able to shake it – the
only thing we have at the moment and again it's for a younger
person is a trainee computer programmer – we could of course
put you on a government sponsored training programme in
either the building or engineering industries – if we get
anything else we'll let you know and remember we're always
only an appointment away – that's a good idea sparky isn't it
the government sponsor you with money which is already
rightly yours to fuck about with lego

you see the guy who was dealing with me his handwriting was
like a child's – he couldn't spell co-ordinate – it's a joke – i
couldn't see under the table but i could feel the vibes drifting
up from his slip-ons – i kept thinking i hope this happens to
you someday kid – i want you to sit in this seat and be
humiliated by some . . . – you're right sparky he's only trying
to earn a living

readies – money money money – what would you think the
chances would be of me walking down a street in new york
and going into one of these take-away places and ordering a
bowl of irish stew or an ulster fry – it's funny that isn't it –
i can cross the street here and buy a big bucket of that kentucky
fried shite though – we start off with pieces of chicken and end
up destroying everything of value – bigger better faster – no
time for people – people are scrubbed stroked off the list of
tasks to complete – potential fulfilling tasks – today was a bad
day i did not fulfil my potential i must see my analyst about
this and make sure he fulfils his potential – and we fall for it –
we're told this is the way to live and eventually we go for it –
i should have taken myself off to the u s of a and opened up a
chain of stew take-aways – and how would you like your stew
sir on a plate or the irish way in a coal bucket on the back of a
donkey – and then i could have a special – buy your child a
mini bucket of stew and you'll get completely free of charge a
small plastic thatched cottage complete with ginger haired
better than her own natural ginger of course maiden colleen
wearing an aran sweater knitted by her drunken granny while
in front of an open turf fire boiling a field and a half of
potatoes – yes and you have a nice day too

why didn't we go to america when we were first married – we
could have been big now in kentucky – the boy'd be in college
now studying golf course management – happy days – i must
talk with him – i need to do that – why don't you go
swimming with mom you might enjoy it – no first name terms
there – i don't like the water it's too wet – water isn't actually
wet – to say water is wet doesn't describe any quality that the
water has – water is wet is inaccurate – water is water – i don't
understand that and that's what's inside his head – water on the
brain – ha ha ha – i don't care about the water forget the water
– i love you – i love you

i can't say it i never could – i've never said those words to
anyone – does that make me a bastard sparky do you think –
emotionally retarded – maybe the boy's right – i'll give you
whatever odds you like the boyos in slip-ons have no problem
saying it – what would you like for breakfast dear – a boiled
egg beat up in a cup and cut the toast into little soldiers –
i love you – i love you too – not as much as i love you – i love
you the equivalent of a citybus full of ballyhornan sand each
grain being an ocean of love – good morning children – oh
wife of mine and mother of my children beat up eggs and
soldiers all round – i love you all

i remember going to the hospital when the boy was born and
holding him in my arms – hannah was sleeping – the three of
us together and i thought i'm happy this is the way it's meant
to be – and then whoosh i'm here – the whoosh factor – i've a
dummy in my mouth then whoosh – i'm playing handball at the
bottom of the street then whoosh – i'm working then whoosh –
i'm married then whoosh – i'm a father then whoosh – i'm . . .
– what am i? – out of touch?

i came straight back to the house after the bookies thing –
folded every sheet every towel washed every dish – sat in this
room turned the tv on – racing epsom – who won the derby in
1966 – you don't know – a lot of good philosophy is boy –
i know though – charlottown 25 may 1966 – a horse called
anglo won the grand national that year – what use is it
knowing that – it's like the chewing gum on the arse of the

trousers – no use – tv off – i couldn't sit in the room the
wallpaper was annoying me – i had to get out – so i got onto a
bus and headed for the nearest swimming pool had a swim and
then had a session on the sunbed – the old sun tan trick

that was a wee joke sparky pets – i went to the pub – i'm there
in the middle of everyone holding court – that's me a bar-room
philosopher – maybe that's where the boy gets it from – the
drink's flying and it's all queen victoria was a lesbian and
knew fuck all about horse racing – on the waterfront was the
best movie every made – the tories are a shower of shite – how
can you walk from here to the albert clock without turning
right – all good stuff – i'm in control there sparky you see –
i know the lay of the land – the pub's like a commune if you
have it you spend it if you don't you'll be looked after – that's
the way things should be if someone's in diffs sort them out –
there for the grace of god go i or whatever – today was
different though – someone had just ordered a drink – we were
arguing about sex before marriage and i said heavy petting's
alright but don't follow through with the old cough rock – they
all started to laugh and it got louder and louder – their faces
getting bigger as if they were going to burst – then it started
happening again – the laughter louder louder – i thought oh
jesus no not here – i've nowhere else to go – it's not that funny
stop laughing – stop the laughing – they're all laughing at me –
gus the joker

it's all racing through my head now – he's a lazy fucker why
doesn't he get a job – he drinks the grocery money you know –
he has it made living off his wife – he's funny like but you
couldn't take him seriously you couldn't trust him with
something important like a job – stop fucking laughing

where do you go when you want to think sparky – do you have
a special place you wander off to and get your act together –
i ended up in the park – i don't know why – i was walking and
then i'm sitting on a bench watching some children playing on
the swings – i thought i'd like to do that why shouldn't i have
a swing it's not a crime – they all looked happy you see –
i thought maybe it's the swinging that's making them happy –
i was half way over to them too – bloody stupid – gus on the

swings – the head has gone it's official – gus mcmahon has finally entered the twilight zone – my da painted the railings round the park – i bet you didn't know that sparky – wee mick the red leader

there was a man knew his place in the world no confusion there – breakfast work dinner paper smoking bed – breakfast work dinner paper smoking bed drunk all weekend – then the same again – never a word out of him too unless he was gargled then he'd curse the world up and down – he was a robot – there's only one thing i ever remember him doing or saying outside his routine – i was about fourteen i was sitting in the house it was a saturday morning – why aren't you out playing handball kid? – i was always playing against the gable wall at the bottom of the street – i was good too – best in the district – i've no one to play with they're all away at a football match – i'll play you – and he did – we must have been down there playing for about two or or three hours – wee mick shirt sleeves rolled up the sweat lashing out of him – it was the only time i ever saw him run or sweat or laugh or slap me on the back and say well done kid – after that it was back to the breakfast work dinner business – one morning's handball and i thought he was a great fella – one morning out of all that time

after my mother died there was just me and him for a while – have you my piece made up kid? – get me twenty woodbine kid – i'm just going for a pint kid – are those shoes polished kid? – grey fucking shoes – a grey man in grey shoes – he died six months after he retired – i was away at a race meeting the curragh or something – i walked into the house nobody there – the coffin was in the parlour – best suit and grey shoes – i took the shoes off and threw them in the bin and put mine on him – grey shoes – they never just looked right – there lived a man and now he's dead and that was it – grey isn't a colour you see sparky – it's bland there's no life in it it says nothing – and i believe you can tell a person by their shoes – well it makes sense to me – we all live our lives by rules and theories we don't understand so why not another one – the gus mcmahon theory of grey shoes – people who wear grey shoes aren't worth a fuck

today was a journey sparky but it didn't end in the park – i
went to the gable wall – i didn't know that's where i was going
but that's where i ended up – there was no one there so i went
to the shop bought a ball and had a game of handball – whack
whack whoosh – well done kid – serve side of the hand high
against the wall it'll go over his head – dad runs backwards
stoops down to his left scoops it up – close the fist smack it
as low as you can – he's running as fast as he can – red face
puffing panting – fist clenched – crack – below the brick –
why are you stopping kid? – that was below the brick – there's
something wrong with your eyes it's my serve give me the ball
what's the score? – ten nine to me – what wins it? – first to
eleven – this is it then – dad serves – out of bounds – you've
another go – he serves high i can get it but i let it go – what's
wrong with you i thought you said you were good at this –
serve – ten all – serves high – whack – it's low whack – high
low low high – whack – whack – whack – low and hard i'm
running for it – i'm going to reach it – it's there – out of the
corner of my eye i see the lamp post – i'm getting close to it
i'm going to smack into it – go for the shot and hit the lamp
post or stop – go for the shot and hit the lamp post or stop – go
for the winner kid – i pull back – stop – hindrance – no chance
kid you could've got it – if you want to win you've got to go
for your shots kid – lying bastard you lying bastard you can't
win anymore

all my shots are out of date now they're playing a new game
and i don't even know the rules – i let you win you see – you
weren't really up to it so i let you win – but they don't do that
anymore – i walked up the street and stood outside my old
house – journey's end – a small dingy wee place – i called at
the door and said to the woman who answered it i used to live
here – i played handball with my father at the bottom of the
street – do you mind if i come in and have a look around –
i just want to see how things have changed – i'm afraid not –
door closed

what was i doing there? – that's what's frightening me sparky
– i'm doing things and i don't know why – all the days from
here on in can't be like this – when i was working i was alright
but now it's all swings paranoia spontaneous deafness and

playing handball with a man that's been dead for twenty
fucking years

you see sparky it's not me i can't handle it life hasn't equipped
me for this – i don't want to delve deep discover things i'd
forgotten unlock all the dreams nightmares guilt longings that
are bedded deep in my mind – that just fucks things up – it's
too late for all that – i've lived a life i'm used to it changing it
won't do me any good – and this is it you see – if my da had
never uttered a word to me in his whole life what difference
does it make to me – i'm a grown man now – what? – i'm
responsible for who i am that's the way it's always been – but
you see sparky when you've time on your hands you start
thinking about these things and everything gets jumbled up –
you start examining yourself and then you look at your family
and think who am i? – who are they? – do they know me do
i know them? – and then you think why are they the way they
are is it my fault? – i can't talk to my son because my father
didn't talk to me – i don't love my wife and she doesn't care
about me because i've been married for thirty years and she
doesn't know i don't like currant squares – that's all bollocks –
not talking talking too much saying the wrong thing saying the
right thing caring not caring loving hating comforting arguing –
that's the way things are i can handle that i understand it

but when you've time on your hands it all becomes something
else – you've nothing to do with your mind so you start asking
questions – the questions become serious – you make up
answers – connect things that aren't connected – then bang
you're knocking at the door of your old house thinking – this
is going to help me everthing's going to become clear i'll
understand – but you don't because it's all to do with today –
now – that's why tomorrow can't be like today something has
to turn up you see or i'll keep asking the questions and it'll
destroy me

is my sparky pets asleep – tomorrow will be different – i'll
take up dancing *(starts to waltz)* one two three one two three –
are you listening you have to listen – one two three one two
three . . .